runt · said deadly, while heavenly fathers · see
stars shaped like memories

AWORDLIKEGOD

leo jenkins

AWORDLIKEGOD:

Said Deadly,
While Heavenly
Fathers
Hunt Stars
Shaped Like Memories

leo jenkins

Publisher: Dead Reckoning Collective
Book Cover Artwork: Leo Jenkins
Book Cover Design: Tyler James Carroll & Leo Jenkins

Printed in the United States of America

ISBN-13: 979-8-9862724-6-7 (paperback)

CONTENTS

A DEDICATION IN QUOTES:

To all those who have written a rung on the ladder of truth, aimed upward toward the divine.

"Time is the seed of the Universe."
-Vyassa

"God is not in might but in truth."
-Fyodor Dostoevsky

"The spiritual nature of reality has been the principle preoccupation of mankind since forever and it's not going away any time soon."
-Cormac McCarthy

"Let me keep my distance, always, from those who think they have the answers."
-Mary Oliver

"Convictions are more dangerous enemies of truth than lies."
-Friedrich Nietzsche

"We have only one story. All novels, all poetry, are built on the never ending contest in ourselves of good and evil."
-John Steinbeck

"Perhaps all wisdom, and all truth, and all sincerity, are just compressed into that inappreciable moment of time in which we step over the threshold of the Invisible."
-Joseph Conrad

"This universe that we know, began in almost absolute simplicity, and it has been getting more complex for about fifteen billion years. In another billion years it will be still more complex than it is now. In five billion, in ten billion—it is always getting more complex. It is moving toward ... something. It is moving toward some kind of ultimate complexity. We might not get there. An atom of hydrogen might not get there, or a leaf, or a man, or a planet might not get there, to that ultimate complexity. But we are all moving towards it— everything in the universe is moving towards it. And that final complexity, that thing we are all moving to, is what I choose to call God. If you don't like that word, God, call it the Ultimate Complexity. Whatever you call it, the whole universe is moving toward it."
-Gregory David Roberts

INTRODUCTION

Hello reader. How have you been? It's been a while. I've been busy working on a new book for you. It is taking longer than expected, but things worth doing often do. This isn't that book, by the way. That book is about life and death, about polarity and reality. But I probably shouldn't use the introduction of this book to discuss another book. That would certainly be a blunder. Except, this book would likely not exist without that other book. You see, I'm attempting to lift a large topic and move it around. If you can keep this between you and me, reader, I'm still developing the technical ability to lay out the subject with clarity over several hundred pages. I get stuck sometimes. I don't mind admitting this to you because we've grown so close over the years, and anyway, we all get stuck at times while working towards our lofty goals. Don't we, reader?

When I struggle to move the cursor, I don't allow myself to become frustrated. No reader, I simply pick up a pen. I write a single word; it doesn't matter what the word is because I am writing. Then, and I hope this isn't saying too much, because maybe it goes a little too deep into my process or whatever you want to call it, but I get out of the way of the pen. That is to say that whatever wants to come out, whatever wants to follow that first word is what fills the page.

Well, over the course of a long year of writing that other book, the one about life and death and the reality of existence, I got stuck a lot. I got stuck so often that after about a year, I noticed that I had filled up a few notebooks with free-verse poems. As I flipped through them one foggy day, I noticed a distinct pattern. They almost all had to do with the nature of reality, the relationship with belief, and the Divine. Imagine that, accidentally writing a book about God. But how else could one write a book about a subject with no borders, no lines, no form, no beginning, and no end? If I were a Jungian, I could attribute this work to my subconscious mind or, perhaps, our collective unconscious. I'm not a Jungian, though. I'm not not a Jungian either. He had a lot of great ideas, after all. So did Jesus Christ, and so did Buddha. So did Albert Einstein and Theodor Geisel.

Without ever asking the question, my hand wrote out the response to three questions. I had pumped my mind full of all these different books over the past eight years trying to prepare myself to write that book, the other book, the book about life and death, existence and belief. Books like The Mahabharata, The Tao, The Holy Bible, and Horton Hears a Who. Hundreds of books bounced around inside my skull for years, each a broken piece, seeking its place in the grand mosaic of truth. Not my truth, reader. Not your truth. But our truth. Not what I believe to be true, but what is true.

Perhaps at times, I misinterpreted what was coming through from the subconscious. In fact, there are cases of that herein. I'm sure I forced a line or two to make it read pretty instead of trusting what was falling out. I'm sure the ego played its part in writing every one of those great books bouncing around in my skull. It can be difficult, as you may know, which voice in your head to trust. What I'm learning, and I don't mind sharing with you, is the more trust I place in the voice that wants nothing, the more harmonious I feel. That harmony tends to echo out.

I'm getting a little off track here, reader. And I hope you forgive me for that. We just haven't had a chance to communicate in such a long while, and if I'm being honest, I've missed you.

Is it strange to you that you've been staring at a flat white sheet of paper, marked with two dozen little symbols repeated in different patterns, and that alone has caused you to think about something or perhaps even feel something? Isn't it wild, reader, the power of symbols—the power of words?

Anyway, I hope you are thriving wherever you are. I hope you are reaching out through trepidation and touching the exquisite experience of being alive, even when it hurts, especially when it hurts. I hope you know yourself, your true self, your true-beautiful-brilliant self. I hope to hear from you soon, reader. I hope to read your words and see your light on display. Write back soon. I promise to be your reader.

Oh yes, the three questions I mentioned. Of course. I didn't mean to skim over that, and you are right; they are of the greatest importance. Please give some time to these questions before moving forward and turning the page. How much time? Well, that depends on you. I can't answer that for you. The longer we spend with these questions, though, the better.

What do I believe?

Where did the belief originate?

Why do I believe what I believe—
What does this belief provide?

With much love and great respect,
-lj

IN THE BEGINNING

Before money
Before government
Before Christ and Muhammed
Before Vishnu and Buddha
Gilgamesh and Achilles
We sat telling stories.

One burning light to unite
We sat telling stories
Sparks rose against the cold night
We huddled, pointed to the heavens
And made gods in our image.

Chasing prey across the cosmos
The first gods were hunters
made of stars, stars made of dust,
dust made of Hydrogen Adams–
made of one positive {+} and one negative {-}.
A universe made of equal, opposite pairs.

IDIOMA

Nature is a language.
Numbers are language.
Words are language.
Emotions are language.
Music is language.
Art is language.
Symbols are language.

The universe is a linguist
And even stars have stars inside of them.
Dialogue is a frog, leaping beneath the skin,
Speaking out about the world within.
Croaking and joking
How we write division.
All things are all things,
Articulations.
All things are all things,
Expressing,
Sometimes screaming,
Leaping from the pages,
But they all have meaning
If you speak the language.

PART I:

From What FORM
Prevails A mind
Which Knows Itself,
Knows God

PAIR OF SOCKS

I've got this pair of socks
That are putting me on–
A long black and short white one.
I've got this life clock chirping
Like a ticking time bomb,
Just a matter of time before
All my rights are wrong.
I've got this heart
That sings like a song–
Melodies of memories yet to come.
I've got this weakness
Where I have to be strong,
Still carrying ghosts long gone.
I've got this God
Who feels more like a paradox
In a pair of socks
Putting me on.

LITTLE THINGS

There is a difference between hearing and understanding
Between empathy and compassion
Between dying from the snakes bite
And its venom.
There's a little known difference between beer and barleywine
That happens around…
15 percent
Of the world's human population is disabled.
Humanity must mean something.
One billion people suffering,
The others sacrificing
To keep the billion living
That may be a little thing,
But it's not nothing.
Hell, a bone breaking used to mean dying,
Still does for many in the wild.

A child's footsteps start
Unsteady
Toward unknown destinations.
My daughter is three and marvels
At the sight of her own steps,
Her footprints,
Her mark on the world.
She walks from flat ground,
Up mountains,
And over oceans—
Past the stars
Into a memory of
Who we are…
Came from who we will be
She can see those little things,
How butterflies flap their wings,
Erratically.
All while navigating perfectly
To destinations never seen.

STILL SPINNING

I tried to find
The end of myself
There was just beginning
Infinite lives intertwined
Still spinning, still suffering.

I clenched fists with this
unwillingness to surrender.
Found the power in pain
And judgment days,
They marched across my
Calendar like a parade.

Make no mistake
I am not ashamed
Of the violence I became
On those trial days—
The ones that made me
Who I became;
A man with scars,
With triumph, with pain
Not a consequence
A GIFT of living
Still giving infinite breath,
Still spinning, still suffering,
Still surviving, apologizing,
And refining the infinite lives,
Still spinning.
Still spinning.

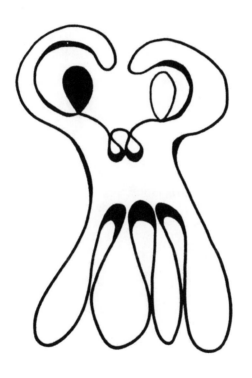

AUTHORITY, MYSTERY, AND MIRACLES

From no word may truth prevail
Marred by joy and her feckless
Mirrored squalor.
No word reigns
Our sleepless hearts
Set adrift in freedom.
No shape but shadow
Of fatherly guidance.

Tremendous undertaking—
Inventing wisdom.
What thumbs hold our pen,
Make our bread,
Bend,
Clasped in
Obedience
To authority, mystery, and miracles.

What rebel cracked our ribs?
Manic laughter in the face of love.
Surrender breathless,
The hot weight of tears.
No joy!
No joy in the rebel's heart.

One word tearing us apart
But freedom
To discover,
Unearth.
            (planting seeds becoming trees we used to be climbing.)
Discovery is blinding.
Pain unknowing
Asking, exploring
In the wild,
Wandering.

                              What roots we cling.
                              What truth we need.

Be apparent
Five senses
Constructing reality.

The truth?
I bleed.
The noose
May need

Tying
To come the black end
Abrupt and in-

Finite.

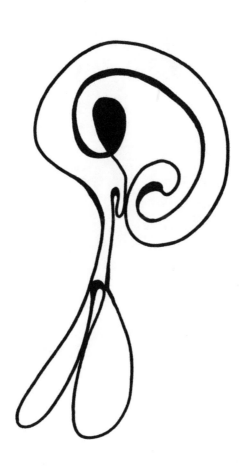

ID

The more I explore
The more I abhor
Myself...

(Keep your suffering)

...is drilling holes into the ceiling
The fissures are feeling
Like the shifting floor
While the core is cracking.
Piano music keeps dancing
And I think of Christ.

(Keep your suffering)

All my life
I sought to feel
A reality beyond
Nervous skin
A light no eye can see
It seems the proding is defining me.

(Keep your suffering)

What gapping mental hole
With drill bit melting
Against iron shells of ego
And insufficiency—
A cracking.

(Keep your suffering)

Inadequacy—the hand that's writing
The mind that's thriving
On duality:
A polar bear in a lava sea,
A dictator of anarchy,
A lamb with lion's teeth.

(Keep your suffering)

Not the intention to question
The king - the deity,
But who cast me into being
With a mind thinking
Critically?

(Keep your suffering)

I am forth, and multiplying
I am flawed
Yet seldom crying
I am a warrior's heart
And a poet's mind

Yet I don't have the time,
The time, the time,
The time has me
Wrapped around its spiraled pinky
And I'm dying
A minute at a time,
A time, a time will come,
A kingdom done
With no king surrendering.

(Keep your suffering)

I could keep going,
Keep drilling,
But what I'd find
Will never mind
The truth of reality
For what is God's face
With no eyes to see
When those eyes
Will shine eventually,
Inevitably, through the darkness
Piercing.
The one thing guaranteed—
Discovery—death awakening.
What plundering
Unconscious collective
Could save us?
What truth has betrayed us
Along our way,
While digging?

(LEAVE YOUR SUFFERING)

THE SOUND OF ORANGE

Through will of torment
What bag of nails
To hold our suffering.
Rejoice and hoist
Solemn past in place
Of present grace,
Deep lines upon a face
Made old by war folly.
In tethered rage
Left bygone days,
No fame,
But worth remembering.
No words explain,
To blame engraven images
Of an innocence devouring.
Plagued skin akin
To humanities immuring.
Golden leaves in the
Autumn of our lives
Stacked high
As bodies rotting.
Celebrate the date
Your life began its ending.
Navigate the straight
Of morality bending.
God's will and
The sound of orange.

EXISTENTIAL SNACKS

I am 40 years old. Existential dread is a playful companion.
The comradery from foreign wars has spread thin.
Listen, my brothers live in different tax codes
and raise children whose names I do not know.
They pay mortgage to banks, keep heads a float,
to sip whiskey when their children's eyes are closed.
They buy new clothes,
shirts with slogans and monikers
reminding them of who they were.
Some of them found Christ,
he was hiding in plain sight.
And despite my disbelief,
Their plight has seen relief.
Still I tease these seasoned
men who preach of certainties,
with no way to disprove their findings.

Sleep is a tease. Even when it works it's a second hand courtesy.
Nothing like the real thing,
a dirt nap, perhaps, could ease this suffering.
I keep seeing these people preaching a cosmic awakening—
drinking ayahuasca—eating peyote—
seeking out meaning, but finding only poetry.
Writing lines disguised like landmines in a mind constantly
questioning if this path will lead to a place worth going, or to
another tourniquet that keeps life from flowing.
I take pity on the healthy. A disease is an enemy worth fighting.
A person in their 30's or 40's with no war is withering. And I have
friends worth remembering who gave their last breath that
prosperity would envelop me. They gave, in their 20's, a gift so great
the weight is unrelenting. I carry it with me to family dinners, and
social gatherings—through airports, from overseas.
It used to be crushing,
but now it makes me happy,
knowing they'll never leave.
My daughter's answer to everything
is, "peanut butter and jelly, please."
If you don't see how that fits into an existential dilemma, keep
reading…

Simplicity makes certainty a possibility.
And even when it's raining
The sun is shining.
Climbing mountains
Is a waste of time.
Joy finds folly
In both sobriety
And wine.
A broad
Perigdime
Is a crime
Worth
Committing.
Even when it leads to diatribes no one finds compelling.
And the answer to everything
Is still, "peanut butter and jelly."

A broken clock's tick tock makes time a triviality
Spirituality, in the wrong hands,
Has never killed a man.
Religion, on the other hand.

But let's pretend
Every point has a beginning
And an end
As all things are supposed to,
Like a sandwich,
The universe,
And the breath in you.
Let's pretend
This isn't something,
We're all living through—
Searching to find a way to calm our mind,
And please our belly.
My three year old figured it out before me.
The meaning of existence is...

PART II:

Five sense
In three dimensions
Make for
Little devils
With ill intentions

THE FLAVOR OF VORTEX

Golden light falls on closed eyes. Black gives rise to amber
horizons. A lone cardinal sings praising the coming morning,
warbling, awakening the shy ones. Muscles have tightened, stiff in
the dawn of four decades bygone unenlightened. Creek-pop, bent,
upright and moving forward, albeit slowly into the frozen morning.
Step-shuffle-step toward the coffee boiling a thin gray ribbon
dancing a scent that brings me back to camping with my dad in
northern Arizona. A fist full of teachers, golden. I grew them in the
light of such similar mornings. Dry now, in they go, twirling, ground
to powder and mixed with citrus. A taste of earth intermixed with the
flavor of vortex. Eyes shift
Seems my left is where my right went.

B   R   E   A   T   H   E
Slow
There ain't no
Con   trol   ling   this.
                        F   O   C   U   S

Form is formless.

Which existence persists beyond the five senses

TWIST

Spiral riding

        Double helix

                Red eyes contrived

                      Of infinite lives

Peering.

Buddha become me

        A sensation oh so settling

                    No words—
                    Pure empathy
                    Leads me
                    To dying

A thousand times

        REBORN

                    Like bubbles
                    In a soap storm
                    Re

        Forming

Dying

RE

Forming

Dying

Re   Forming

Dying

Re

Forming

Until dying
Becomes boring

Now my eyes are among them
The infinite-

The one-

Zen-

Tao word without definition-

The serpentine line between

Yang and Yin.

With them I see the necessity of we.
I see

where we are going, where we are from
is where we will always be

I see
The shape
Of the taste
Of the sound
Of the seed

I see
Beyond the up
The down
And in between

I see
Without eyes
The sunrise waking me.

POISON

Journeys of unknown destinations,
Like places without faces
Covered in malaise.
The days play with
Pliable emotions.
We had a choice,
To heed the voice within,
Or bow to consumerism,
And we bought all in!
Denied conditions of growth
Through suffering,
Believed suffrage
Was freedom.
We leapt at these prosperities;
Cheap screens, and fruits from foreign regions.
But the screen I've seen
Is screaming for reasons yours isn't even seeing.
Go on believing division is a form of altruism—
That you haven't been conditioned
From the moment this journey began,
So long as you're plugged in and buying
You belong to them!
Hear me
More
Is your
Poison.
The antidote is a journey
With no destination.

The ones who WOKE
Ain't broadcasting.
They're beneath a tree, breathing.
Or walking s l o w l y toward the possibility of infinite reality.
A seed which began this journey
And a wheel that keeps us turning.

So rare is he who bleeds without believing.
Yet the truth no one seems to be selling
Is a journey with no beginning.

Remember, when the bass drum kicks it's
Time to clap along.
Remember,
Your place
Your race
And all
You've done wrong!

Remember, the face with no place before they are gone.
There is grace, there is grace in their song.

Remember, to you this breath belongs.
So breathe necessarily, your own resuscitation

Believe,

HERE is the journey

NOW is the destination.

DEAR GOD IN HEAVEN

Dear God in Heaven,
Forgive me
The time I forgot
The poetry
Of living becomes a heavy thing,
So much to carry.

Golden light singing
Through silent leaves
Memories amassing—
Amusing
A devil's plaything.
Shadow puppets
Dance from
Noose strings.
Responsibilities,
The clamor
Of key rings.
Never knowing,
Forego exploring,
Pad the coffers,
Ignore the day-dreams.
Bloody fingers scratching
At coffin inseams.
It seems
So melancholy
Dear God,
In heaven,
Without poetry.

HIKURI

Thin twigs ignite
Long strips of dark hardwood
Interlaced in a V-shape.

Voices chatter,
Bouncing light laughing,
Conversations amid the coming

Stars.
Alters set—white roses
—dark chocolate.

A feather fans the flame
Flapping sends sparks against
The crisp night air.

Picking red embers with cautious
Fingers, tossed in, then, stretched
Leather across the drum.

Ten gallon cauldron, in flame.
The holy man
Mix the medicine.

Eleven scoops of powder added
To the boiling cauldron.
Stir, stir, stir.

The steam rising
Gray into the night.
A cell phone for light.

A rattle and a drum.
The wise one
Says a prayer.

The grandmother
And grandfather
Are here.

A cleanse : A mark
Hey-Ya-Na-Way-No-Eh-Hum
A rattle : A drum

A staff and rattle pass
Yah-Wah-Nah-Ho-Yah-Wah-Nay-Nas

A rattle : A drum
The coals glow, plump
Spirits dance in shadows.

All words seep inside.
A rattle : A prayer
We-Awah-Hey-Nee-Hay.

NEON HIGHWAYS

I watched goats graze
Along highways.
I spent forty days
In silence, speaking
Words of defiance
Against the science of God.
No shepherds on those streets,
Bloody feet gone walking.
A soul with leprosy
Leaving pieces of bloody
Dogma and serenity
Aching to breath.
Listless from lethargy
The mountain, ascending
The task, unending,
But what the goats
Don't know is
The drivers been drinking
From a cup overflowing
with Karma and Ecstasy.

Show me the bones
Bleached in new beginnings,
The hollow ones repurposed
For beating
On war drums,
Or drinking from,
In the desert hallucinating
About goats tied by shoe strings,
Tied to feet gone walking
Without moving.

I died three times
That night beneath
The piercing light
Of moon beams.

The fire cracked
And there I sat
Still peering
Through reality seams.

A vision of me,
Though trembling,
A panther breaths
Engaged in awakening.

The goats all flee
The light it seems
Is rising
Endlessly.

The son, it seems
Is alive and rising
The almost dreams
Can die now, peacefully.

Like goats on highways
Run down needlessly
By drivers high on peace
And prosperity.

GONE WALKING

When the wind blows cold
Old shoes go on walking.
Talking fast is fatal in the
Sleet and sideways rain of
Allegory and fable. The cradle
Of civilization rocking in
Treetops whose branches touch
Heaven, whose roots transcend
The seven layers of sin.
Soil fertilized by prideful men
Sowing boundary lines of nations
Invading language, culture, and education.
A symbol ascends,
A purpose greater than skin
Condemning sensation.

Broken homes still burning
White phosphorus indiscriminate, incinerating
The pious and righteous
Both scream for salvation–
No rain can save the skin.
But feet meet street,
Keep on walking.
Homes are for building.
Stones are for hurling.
Pick up and move
The storm is swirling
In the hearts of man.
Indecision is thunder roiling.

Hold your ground
So your child may dig
Your place beneath it.
What holy soil
In our veins so stagnant
Where best friends are buried
Beneath trees toppled by the tempest.

She took her first steps in that kitchen
Where bricks and broken glass
Rob the best of us.
What memories are worth drowning for?
What war is worth our feet, our dreams
Our children?
What feast awaits the man gone walking?

MOON ROCKS

Look!
There's a room
Made of moon rocks
Where clocks have
No value.
I've been there,
Where circles are made of squares,
Where red hairs
On trilobites bite
Through shadows of
Past versions of you.

The room is not a room
It's a tomb cut in two
Different places,
Mirroring integration.
A window in the face of
The mason stacking rocks
Made of you,
Made of moon,
Made of egos
You're passing through,
To other sides of consciousness.
An ape acting as evolution's therapist,
Asking questions so preposterous–
(Who and why)
Instead of how & when.
Was sin given more weight
Than a social construction?

If we're on this spin,
We may as well, might begin
To look at archetypes,
Wearing thin.
A God-King ascending,
A child pretending,
They found a hero within.

But that veil is a snail
Made of circles,
Made of squares,
Made the fundamental

Seem sophomoric and if
You care to explore it,
There's a room made
Of moon rocks,
Don't knock,
There's no door to it.

If you've ever been
You know the ceiling
Is where the floor went
Space and time are no more a fabric
Than simple elastic
On a garment so fantastic
It wears itself
To dinner parties,
And the origin of species—
A bang gone galactic.

And if that seems thick,
Don't remove the brick
In the back of the room.
Behind is a hall so small
It begins and ends with all
The rooms made of moon rocks,
Made of free thought,
Made of conditioning strings,
Dancing puppets through "reality"
But the hand is yours
Call it duality,
Or divinity,
I'm unsure,
I just swallowed the key.

Bitter angels
Seem to stay

WHERE

Better angels
Fly away

ABOVE ALL, DON'T LIE TO YOURSELF

I lied—
But only to myself.
Imagine the surprise
I felt
When every little thing
Offended me so easily.

Hell made in mistruth
Virtue—signaling
Legs spread involuntarily
as dissonance deafening.

I raped
But only myself.
Imagine the surprise
I felt
When every little thing
Gave rise to victimizing.

I tried,
But never past myself.
Imagine the surprise
I felt
When every little thing
Remained feeble and unfelt.

BROTHER'S KEEPER

I fear I failed, Oh God,
My brother at my table
Hands clasped with judging heart
Head bowed, he lacked humility
I triumphed in civility. I failed
To see
The person screaming. A hell devised of lies
In seething agony. I failed
To hold
His suffering, masked of course,
In fleeting whispers of insecurity while yelling,
"Look at me! My bravery! The badge I carry!"
Self-vengeance and apathy
Broken over bread risen from a devil's yeast,
Yet it was I who failed to rise,
To keep my brother, solemnly.
So I bow and ask forgiveness, please.

PART III:

We

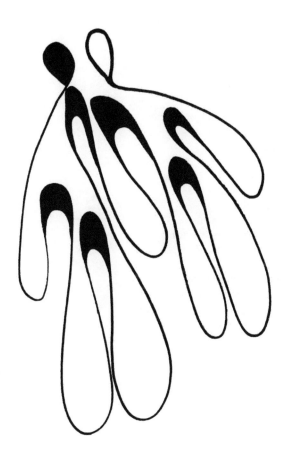

GIVE

Give me a song
That sings me to sleep.
Hum me a moment
Like human in need,
Believing
I, You, We, were always
Meant to be
A part of these things,
These self-perceived
Tragedies.

Give me belief
To ease the jagged
Parts of living.
Give me division,
Something to press against,
To sharpen the steel of belief.

Give me stedfast knowing
In place of empathy,
Where living is easy.
Give me the dying
Where truth lives.
Give me the moment
Impervious
To rhetoric
Give me the ease,
The tragedy.
Give me the pain,
Give me the we.

WHAT WE WIELD

Can you allow the sound
To play your ear like a drum?
Did you run to the sound of guns?
How profound now, to turn from the strum of
Love.

Can you feel a knee that kneels
To some unknown above—
So below—
You laid your friends in rows
Fed them tears for years
Now green grass grows.

Have you exposed
Your eyes to the violent lies
Of reality?
Seen the machine
Where human used to be?

Is it fun to run your tongue across inequity?
To taste the place where demons sleep?

Will you smell the heat
Of conformity
Sit snorting the flame of clever advertising
And anxiety?

Or reveal the veil,
Commence the piercing,
Create something worth more than selling?
Dispel the wheel that keeps us turning.
Rolling over a hundred years—
Is NO TIME on the forever clock of divine
Reality.
Perched high in a dream
We woke still sleeping
The dream became one
THE STRUM
THE LOVE
Was beyond destruction
What may come
From death

Is a blessing
And what we wield
Is the POWER of HEAVEN!

HOW RARE

Spending, saving. Commiserating
Searching for meaning
Is pleasure seeking
Bending reality with thinking
Of dreams we seem
To be living
Writing, reading. Journaling
Taking drugs, but nothing's working.
Life is still thriving and dying
Civilization is still climbing to unknown
Heights despite mythic warnings.
How boring is war
That the gore has gone exploring
For the softer petals
Of brighter mornings?
The love we share is a dare to find meaning,
As rare as a life in a distant galaxy
Surrounded by a Dyson sphere
My dear, my dear,
It's all right here
That time we sat silent, smiling
And bought nothing.
Perhaps now, the drugs are working
The dopamine
The serotonin
The soft sound of you breathing
Into the night, into the stars
That made you who you are.
FOURTEEN BILLION YEARS
Your atoms and mine
Intertwined in a paradigm of circle
A dance unimaginable
Amid the chasm of space and time
If we only knew
How rare is the air
That carries the words,
I   LOVE   YOU.

NEAR SIGHTED

I tried to see
The blooming,
The humming
Bee laboring,
Creating honey.
The smell of
Floral sweet.
The taste of
Fruit that was
Once a seed,
Its roots now
Running deep.
The rays,
The rain
Giving
All we'll ever need.
But all I seemed to see
Was the same sorry,
And paltry weed.

IN THE GARDEN

It's been raining in the mountains
It's been flooding down below
I've been in the garden
Reaping what I've sown—

Picking fruit from trees we planted
Tasting what we could have known
I've been sitting in the shade
So long my roots have made a home

The drifter long departed
The warrior put away
The teacher and the scholar
Are not long here to stay

Move toward mediation
Through the ego and the self
From destruction to creation
To unified-mental-health

Embrace the mediation
Through the shadow to the self
From destruction to creation
To divine and lasting wealth

Taste the fruit we planted
Waste not another day
Swallow hole the seeds of life
They'll guide you on your way

Taste the fruit you planted
Remove the shame of what has been
Swallow hole the seeds of life
to see yourself again in...

The garden.
In the garden.
In the garden.

Knowledge born of nature
In the garden
By a fable we were taken
from the garden
Return now, able, unforsaken
To the garden
To the garden
Unify
In the garden
In the garden
Embrace your shaman
In the garden
In the garden
In the garden

ALONE IS A MALLEABLE CONCEPT

The man stood alone on a train platform at midnight smelling like lost wars, and bourbon, and unrequited love. The clock above mocked a reminder that nothing is granted, life only seems harder for the romantic, and home is a malleable concept. He stood, not feeling anything. He stood beside a dream he was having. His bones were still his own, but his thoughts became commodities, bought and sold like coffee, like trees, like division from media companies.

He couldn't stop what he had seen but there were worse things; like, the data industry, and doing chest compressions on a friend dying.

He tried to wake but couldn't take the reality. His bones were still his own but he'd lost all connection with his family. He reached for living, knowing suffering is at least something. In fact, it's a common bond among the others he had not seen, standing alone, on the crowded platform, at midnight.

BEAUTY AND SUFFERING

If I may…
I'd like to share this dilemma I'm having.
Has a lot to do with beauty
And suffering.

Which, if you think about it,
Is kinda the same thing.

Like, a foreign seed in the desert, struggling,
Breaking free from arid conformity
Informally becoming a tree
Which shades a community
(With poetry)
And from whose leaves come tangerines
That would never taste as sweet
Without the suffering.

I digress,
What's on my chest is how to express
A being so mesmerizing that a simple
Song she sings becomes the dream
We're all living.

I wanna scream,
"Hold high your suffering!"
It's breathing life in me!
And not just me,
But everyone it's touching
You blessing
You holy gift
You gypsy queen!

I mean…
How do you write a thing…

I mean…
What comes to mind initially
Is some troupe about a tree
Yet, the more I'm reflecting
Perhaps it's two roads intersecting
Still, beauty & suffering.

On one road is a MacTruck outta control
That carries love like a load
And the other is a road where
A heart's on a stroll,
Just, smelling the roses
Composing little melodies
Like tangerines,

And, I know, I've used
This device already
But bear with me
That soft heart never saw it coming!

That love truck struck the heart
So Oblivious!
A kind word—
A soft kiss.
A bliss
Unrequited
Is misery—a dilemma.
But a dilemma is an opportunity
For self-discovery
For art and imagining overcoming
It's the divine comedy
Written like a tragedy
Its life, it's love
Its beauty
from suffering.

WHEN HEAVEN CAME

I was on the porch
Fixing an old chair.
She was there
In the garden,
Planting a seed.
Our daughter
Handed us
Each a flower
From a tree
We planted together
And told me,
"It smells like
Strawberries in
The sunshine."

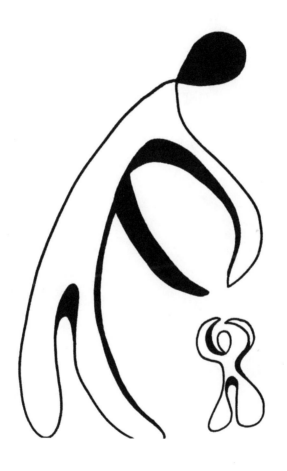

A WORD LIKE LOVE

Love is a word like rock,
I placed into my pocket,
Pulled out a language
Filled with sounds
Shaped like profits.

I evolved those rocks
Into rockets
Hurled them at
Prophets of peace.

I was in need
Of unity
Still screaming,
"You versus me."

We spoke to the stars,
With feeble hearts.
Then fell apart
From silence above.

The moon just laughed at
What an ape I was,
Throwing rocks,
Shaped like love.

KILLER BEES

I've been sleeping inside a machine that runs on dopamine.
I've been dreaming terrifying things
Like the vibrations from freedom's ring
Smothering children.

Been seeing what's coming,
A cloud overcoming the senses
Leaving the crowd
Depressed, anxious, & defenseless
From birds of prey
Circling relentlessly.
I've seen the way
Things can be
Those same vibrations
Humming harmony
Of everlasting liberty,
But none among us is free
If one child is dying from preventable disease
Or starvation from poverty.

So I threw the screen
Woke suddenly from the shattered dream
Came stumbling to see

Where the ruckus was
Swarmed the bees
Like Marines,
Like orchestrated anarchy,
Like the streets
Of burning cities
We freed,
Like aphrodite naked
In the euphrates
Then laid out
Under olive trees,
Like corpses of
Ten thousand babies,
Like the start
And end of history,
Like an unheard plea,
Like We, the swarm,
Like the bees.

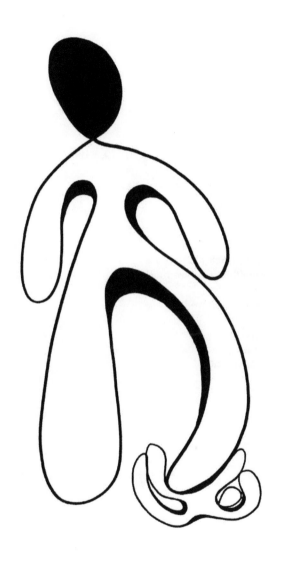

LET ME BE DIVINE

Write me in your afterlife
Let me be divine
Fill me up with stories
Changing over time
Let me soothe your broken
And fuse your fractured spine
Let me break this mold we made
Let me hear you cry
Let me see the truth we hold
Let me be divine
Let me spend your golden calf
Let me change your mind
Let me hold your hand, with love
Let me be divine

THE HOWLING MADNESS

We—the howling madness
Partake in our own devouring
Clamor for resource, abundant
Gather towers of ash and time
display—in marvel—imagination.

A shadow cast—a shadow past
Our dwelling of concrete and ambition
Roiling fear, amygdala recession.

No longer the hunted
We—the trampled,
Howling madness
Partake in our own devouring.

PART IV:

Who
Does
God
Serve

If we are made in their image–
THE CREATOR
–Shouldn't we be
Creating more

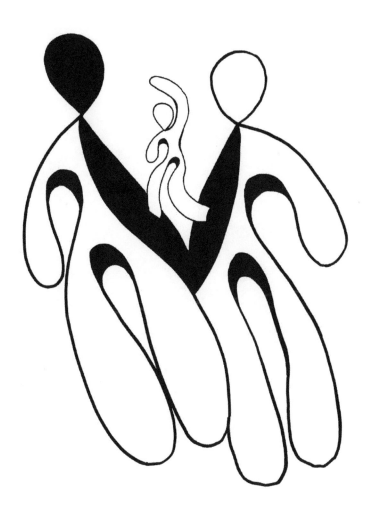

TRUTH DOESN'T NEED A TITLE

Finding meaning
in the mundane
is one thing,

But selling salvation
To a following
is disgusting.

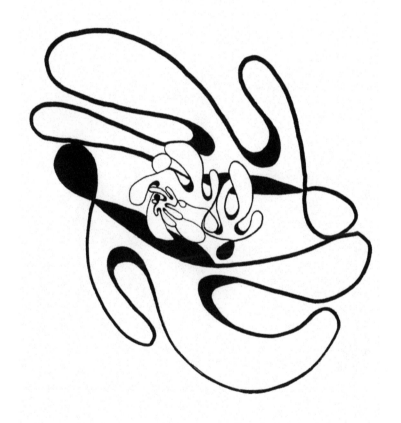

NERVE ENDING

One golden leaf,
Still holding,
Resilient in the breeze,
Faithfully clutching
The swaying tree,
Surrounded by
Youthful green.

Inevitably is falling.
Joy is evolving—
The nature of nurturing.
My leaf, MY GOD,
You were a seed!

What will your carbon be
After a time spent composting?
Your soil gives rise to the wheat,
The bread we knead.

These fingers, deep, with feeling.

Who am I to tell you what a poem means?
The creator?
No, a conduit—
An exposed nerve ending.
Experiencing, connecting,
Embracing sensation.
Blistered, burning.
Learning agony.
Not the price we pay
For joy, overflowing
But the purpose placed
Between the forefinger
And eternity.
When you feel,
You're not just living
You are transmitting
(I see you, seeing me)
An ocular nerve ending.

Poetry is but a tear falling.

There is no explaining divinity—
There is no comprehending
The brain
When you're a nerve ending
Falling
From a tree.

THE BREATH

I am the calm
I am the storm
I am the lynched
I am the horde
I am the wound
I am the sword
I am the breath
bound to this flesh
I am the failure
The lesson
The victory
The test
I am the womb
I am the breath
I am the all
I am what's left
I am ascending
I am the breath
I am connected
Through love
Beyond death
I am the joy
I am the breath
I am tiny
I am immense
I am the knowing
I am the breath

BOOKSHELVES

I have this votive candle on my bookshelf. The wax is red and
wrapped in glass. The glass is clear and wrapped in the holy image
of Kurt Vonnegut, his sacred heart on display.
When I approach the shelf and light the candle it is often because I
am looking for an answer to an unknown question, something
ancient, wisdom hidden amid the worn brown pages. My fingers
walk from spine to spine and his eyes follow me. "Go on," they say,
and my fingers begin moving.
Mary Oliver whispers a dwindling summer creek amid the god of
dirt. MY! What NOW we have, before the bend of Dreams. I believe,
I believe. And the sacred heart glows. What a moment,
Interrupted,
By the belch of Charles Buowski. He's picking at a hemorrhoid—
unafraid
Of blood, or shit, or dirt under the fingernails. Or sloth, or sin of any
sort. He is happy, whatever that means, in the muddy shit. Though
he cries at night, cheap whiskey tears which fall on the keys of an
old typewriter, clack, clack, clacking, the words into the night. At the
first agonizing light of morning a rose is often blooming, thorn
covered and bent, yet rich and honest as the fertilizer and rain from
which it grew.
And a song bird sings, blue
& longing.
Something somber
Like spring
Awe-inspiring
And melancholy.
Lust dripping,
Lyrical pornography.
My eyes shift
Unknowing
If desire is coming
Or going
I smile and admire
The words of Leonard Coheen.
Beneath him
Is RH Sin
Not saying much of anything.

Now Kurt is smiling
Like a grandfather admiring
His fumbling youth, guiding
The heart, the long way to truth.

I hear a war drum beat
The feet of brothers marching,
Who make the world's worst enemies;
Cokie invoking divinity, a Rose with a nose for anarchy and
philosophical inquiry, Geraldo Mena singing praise for pineapple
grenades and the days when the shape of our faces remained
unchanged by whiskey, women, and reflection.
What war we fought with introspection.
Like Tim O'Brien
Defining what weight we carry
Even Kurt's eyes agree
Tim's work is poetry.

"Well," Kurt said to me, "now you're on a course. Keep following.
Keep falling in love with the words of comedic tragedy, repeating.
But be sure to bring yourself to each story."

I read through his light
Despite the waning bliss
Eyes tired, he broke the silence,
"If this ain't nice, what is?"
A kind reminder for a kind of mental shift
Away from war and all its bloody pieces.

There's a shelf marked religion,
But the pages are so stained with division
I can hardly read them
So I stumbled into fiction
But where to begin?
I'm such an infant.
I find my Similac in Jack Kerouac
And take to drinking
Sleeping near a railroad track
Outside of Denver
Alive with jazz culture,
man.
The off-beat
And
Broken
Down. The come back around
And
Dump your heart out,
Kid.

Come meet the tempest.
The fury of words so pure
They hurt your eyeballs
Kid.
A life lived—in loving defiance, and handed
To a generation.

But who came before him?
I went exploring
through Hemingway—
Brilliant—terse—masculinity.
Yet, something was missing.
Fitzgerald could sing
A bit more Victorian,
Floral notes of spring, rising.
But who inspired them?

On the floor, I lay dying,
Prying into Faulkner's mind
And one line sticks
"My mother is a fish."
How will I compare to this?
And Kurt is smiling,
"Keep going. Keep dying."

On the shelf where Hunter S. Thompson sits
Is a jar with tabs in it.
"No, no," said Vonnegut
"If you want to trip
Forget the LSD,
Try the top shelf,
Fydor Dostoyevsky."

My God, in heaven, the clarity.
What a gift to humanity.
Such power displaced with simplicity.
I mean, what an azimuth for the youth.
Just listen, "God is not in might, but in truth."
And if you want to know what truth is
He said, "Active love is labor and perseverance."
A man who wore more than seven years of the cruelest experience,
and brought forth a depth of which even the oceans are oblivious.

Beautiful, but what am I to do with this?
Candle Kurt, give me some guidance
Light the way, deliver me from blindness.
His eyes seemed disappointed (and fading)
I kept searching, fearful.
Too many voices to get to
Brilliant minds like Cormac McCarthy
and Olga Tokarczuk.
Even still a bit dim compared to,
"God is in truth."

I pulled the words' first root.
A hero's journey
Stamped in clay
766,000 days
Before the good book.
A quick look
revealed… a bit of plagiarism.

The Tao, The Vedas, The Kybalion.
Wasn't sure if I was seeking or avoiding Him.
Read the Mahabharata and Thich Nhat Hanh,
From Carl Jung to Spiderman,
Aristotle and the Brothers Grimm.
Should've listened when
Bradbury was burning them.
I got lost somewhere between
Herman Melville and Shel Silverstein
To find myself right back at the beginning.

And the red wax, now liquid.
The black wick burnt, and reminiscent,
Of a melting—like human & divinity—
Etched in poetry,
And prose.
Until the light dies,
So it goes.

A WORD LIKE GOD

God is a word
Like HISfarkaboom
Far and wide
Spring in bloom

God is a word
Like displacate
Astronauts that
Talk like apes

God is a word
Like Granfalloon
The best of us
Gone too soon

God is a word
Like slabhaferkrill
The heart is beating
The mind is still

God is a word
Like Empanourishmade
Arcing light through
A heavy shade

God is word
Like Geo-psyco-metric
The limb is asleep
But still connected

God is a word
Like Konggrillaseed
An interconnectedness
Of all living things

God is a word
Like Foobooterness
The root, branch, and seed
Of consciousness

God is a word
Like Tearfilledeyes
The strongest men
Know how to cry

God is a word
Like FazelWoop
How splendid just
To taste the fruit

God is a word
Like Wetransmutate
Shapes and colors
Form a face

God is a word
Like splendiferous
The serpentine line
Between order and chaos

God is a word
Like spuneffErKiss
The taste of chocolate
Just past the lips

God is a word
Like PlataToot
A naked man
In a 3 piece suit

God is a word
Like Fudderwack
The only front
Without a back

God is a word
Like Allmadeup
The realest thing
You can never touch

God is a word
Like Kerzeekit
Once you have
You can't unsee it

God is a word
Like Simplication
Still trying to work
Here while on vacation

God is a word
Like Mañanakin
Even buildings built by babble
Won't prevail to keep us in

God is a word
Like ॐ

More of a tone
A melody
A rhythm
Like serenity
A frequency, interconnecting
Neglecting not a thing
A non verbal language
Spoken eternally
A voice so sweet and comforting—
A mother whispering dreams
Shaped like allegories to her children, naive and sleeping beneath
a blanket made of stars and stories and when one wakes they can't
help believe that the puzzle piece that was their dream is the
mother's body, entirely. And as we've often seen, just one piece is
peace for a child suffering. A shape can feel so comforting amid the
daunting task of awakening.

It seems to me we should connect our dreams.
It seems to me we can bend those shapes into poetry,
But who am I to tell you what the word means,
When I myself am just now waking.

EPILOGUE

In the end—
The beginning

MOSAIC

One can never be
Without acquiring
Pieces from others.
Each belief borrowed from
Fathers-mothers-sisters-brothers,
Who all observe strangers.
With each interpretation
The scene subtly changes.

An old man takes his final breath.
How unoriginal dying is.
Yet the black tile changes the image.
The space between the notes,
Make the music what it is.
No way to know what comes after all this.
But I have confidence
It's made of colors, shapes, and spaces.
Like living—a mosaic.

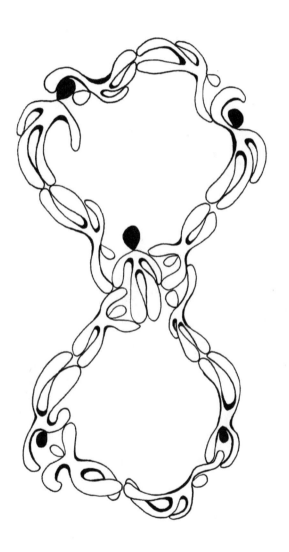

AN EXCERPT FROM WORKS FORTHCOMING:

"Where am I?"

There was no answer and she could not tell if she had asked this question out loud or in her head. There was silence, not the silence of being alone on a cold morning reading to the sound of one's heart, but a complete silence, a void. As this occurred to her, it also occurred that all of her senses were just as absent, dark as the vacuum of space. The nothingness was pure. Overwhelming. She grasped for connection, searched for a thought, a memory. She found nothing, felt nothing. There was no despair in this nothingness, neither was their comfort. In such a state she remained suspended, and yet for a time she could not determine. As though even time had abandoned her, as distant as the notion of distance itself.

"What is this?"

She recognized the voice which asked the question. It rose from a central location, a familiar place. When the answer came, it came from a similar place, and yet The Voice had a different quality. Neither masculine nor feminine, yet both at once. Neither internal nor external from where the question rose. The Voice could be hers, but she did not hear it, she simply understood the response, which was as bright and vibrant a vision as it was a word, a felt-sense, a clear understanding beyond the entanglement and limitation of language.

The constraints of language, the language which has been given, handed down through the ages and used to express burning shades of energy – emotion – had dissolved away in the floating void, so that when The Voice formed a shape, the shape was made of myriad symbols, all of which, perfectly familiar. And The Word formed of myriad symbols was a warm vibration, and she understood and was unafraid. The Word was a source of comfort, much like a child's first blanket.

There was no desire to understand more than The Word, and so there was no struggle. She surrendered to this nirvana, and so The Voice continued, yet in such a soft way that it would not have been understood at all had she so much as held on to a thought.

The Voice passed through her and she understood:

This cannot be after. After requires a before and during. Death requires life as light requires dark.

The symbol of a tilting scale of justice came to her. One side drooping with the weight of bad deeds and evil thoughts, the other side high on righteousness. And The Voice laughed, warm and gentle, then continued.

You are as incapable of good as you are capable of evil. For these are words contrived of beliefs, beliefs manufactured and managed. The Word is balanced. Though half of existence is positive, the other half is negative. This is the quality of The Word. And so judgment is superfluous. As one hand pushes, the other pulls. To judge or punish by removing either does nothing for the whole.

Ascension as reward, dissension as punishment, perpetuates imbalance. Though some teach this system, it exists merely as a device to maintain social order among the juvenile.

And she understood that every action, every thought, is counterbalanced by an equal and opposite action or thought, though the reaction is nearly never seen, nor heard, nor felt. And in this way chaos is, was, and always will be a perfect harmony of balance.

The final flicker of the last light of a universe is the banging spark of the next.

The image of a Circle arose as though the Voice had chosen a shape.

She too had a shape, a dot, just outside the great Circle, infinitesimally small and rapidly shrinking to the extent that the Circle began to appear to warp into the shape of an oval, and then appeared so massive that she could see It only as an infinite wall. Yet she continued to shrink or It continued to grow, so inconceivably immense, stretching out in every direction until It appeared as an interconnected structure made of infinite vibrating pixels.

She observed herself as a pixel. Now she felt as if it were her first sensation. It was the intense feeling of separation from the flowing torrent of pixels. The need for connection, an overwhelming force. The twitch, the vibration of attraction. The space between, as near as infinite.

From the wall, whose boundless pixels lept and danced and bounced off of one another, came forth two, one positive and one negative. The force of their attraction eased the intensity of her oscillation. Until the three touched.

At the instant of connection a light, sharp and bright shot forth, forming a horizon.

From that spot where her dot met theirs at the Great Circle, descended two vast lines, opening evenly at exactly a 60 degree angle. The lines traveled outward, beneath the horizon line, beneath the Great Circle. For months they traveled before eventually sharply turning, each at a 60 degree angle, and meeting.

The form complete.

She recognized the voice. It rose from a central location, a familiar place. The voice wailed, incapable of words. She felt cold and afraid, trembling. The light was intense and burning, though her eyes were closed.

She recognized the voice, one which previously came from a central location, now outside of her, a voice she had thought was her own. The voice gave her comfort as it spoke, gentle and warm as a blanket, "Hello, Sophia. We are so happy to finally meet you, little one."

PREVIOUSLY PUBLISHED WORKS BY DEAD RECKONING COLLECTIVE:

FACT & MEMORY by: Tyler Carroll & Keith Dow

IN LOVE... &WAR: THE POET WARRIOR ANTHOLOGY VOL. 1

WAR... &AFTER: THE POET WARRIOR ANTHOLOGY VOL. 2

WAR{N}PIECES by: Leo Jenkins

LUCKY JOE by: Brian Kimber, Leo Jenkins, and David Rose

SOBER MAN'S THOUGHTS by: William Bolyard

KARMIC PURGATORY by: Keith Dow

WAR IS A RACKET by: Smedley Butler

THE FIRST MARAUDER by: Luke Ryan

WHERE THEY MEET by: Cokie

POPPIES by: Amy Sexaur

ROCK EATER by: Mason Rodrigue

REVISION OF A MAN by: Matt Smythe

ON ASSIMILATION by: Leo Jenkins

SANGIN, THEN AND NOW by Neville Johnson

UPCOMING PUBLICATIONS BY DEAD RECKONING COLLECTIVE:

PHANTOMS by: Ben Fortier

CARMEN ET ERROR by: Moises Machuca

COLLECTIVE

DEAD RECKONING COLLECTIVE is a veteran owned and operated publishing company. Our mission encourages literacy as a component of a positive lifestyle. Although DRC only publishes the written work of military veterans, the intention of closing the divide between civilians and veterans is held in the highest regard. By sharing these stories it is our hope that we can help to clarify how veterans should be viewed by the public and how veterans should view themselves.

Visit us at:

deadreckoningco.com

@deadreckoningcollective

@deadreckoningco

@DRCpublishing

LEST WE FORGET: A RANGER MEDIC'S STORY

A rare look inside the experience of an Army Ranger medic. The compelling true story of what it takes to become and work as a special operations combat medic during the height of the global war on terrorism.

ON ASSIMILATION

Some wars won't end. Some wounds won't heal. Some bonds can't be broken.

Former U.S. Army Ranger medic, Leo Jenkins, picks up where he left off with his best-selling book, Lest We Forget, to explore the difficulties of reintegrating back into society after years at war. In what has been called one of the most important books ever written on transition, Jenkins lays it all on the line one more time with, On Assimilation: A Transition From War.

FIRST TRAIN OUT OF DENVER

Leo has a decision to make—maintain a comfortable position in a career he's no longer passionate about—or take a massive leap of faith. Giving up everything he's ever known, Jenkins sells his business, purges every possession that won't fit into a single backpack and sets off around the world in pursuit of answers.

WITH A PEN

Raw, Evocative, Intelligent; With a Pen is whiskey infused poetry that sheds light on love and war. Leo steps away from prose to poetry to deliver the uncensored truth of his human experience.

WAR{N}PIECES

Fifteen years of reflection, of death and triumph, of struggle and overcoming. war{n}pieces is a poetic journey from war, through love to redemption.

Follow Leo Jenkins

leo-jenkins.com

@leo_jenkins

@Leo_Jenkins_

LEO JENKINS seldom writes in the third person, when he does it's for an author bio, when he doesn't it's for LEST WE FORGET, ON ASSIMILATION, FIRST TRAIN OUT OF DENVER, WITH A PEN, and WAR{N} PIECES.

Leo tells people he is 5' 11" when it's clear to see he's an even 6'. He lies about other things too, like his honesty, his modesty, and his penchant for rare Fabergé eggs.

Leo Jenkins can do this all night.

Leo Jenkins is currently spinning 1532 kilometers per hour on a tiny space rock with eight billion of his closest friends, his amazing partner Lauren, and inspiring daughter Kezia.

CPSIA information can be obtained
at www.ICGtesting.com
Printed in the USA
BVHW061259070323
659880BV00020B/738

9 798986 272467